Tom and Bella are on holiday. They are looking in the rock pools on the beach.

Bella sees a shell moving across the bottom of the pool. 'Tom, Tom,' she shouts. 'Come here.'

Tom goes to look. 'It's a hermit crab,' he says. He scoops it out of the water with his net.

Bella watches Tom drop the hermit crab in her bucket. She goes to look in another pool.

She sees something different move in this pool. 'Tom, Tom,' she shouts. 'Come here.'

Tom goes to look. 'It's a big crab,' he says. 'I'll catch it with my net.'

Tom scoops the crab in his net, but it gets tangled. He can't get it out of his net.

'I'll help,' says Bella. She tries to get hold of the crab, but it grabs her finger. 'Ow, let go, let go!'